D0771395

Apes and Monkeys

Michael and Jane Pelusey

 **Marshall Cavendish**
Benchmark
New York

This edition first published in 2009 in the United States of America by Marshall Cavendish Benchmark.

Marshall Cavendish Benchmark
99 White Plains Road
Tarrytown, NY 10591
www.marshallcavendish.us

First published in 2008 by
MACMILLAN EDUCATION AUSTRALIA PTY LTD
15–19 Claremont Street, South Yarra 3141

Visit our Web site at www.macmillan.com.au or go directly to www.macmillanlibrary.com.au

Associated companies and representatives throughout the world.

Library of Congress Cataloging-in-Publication Data

Pelusey, Michael.
    Apes and monkeys / by Michael and Jane Pelusey.
    p. cm. — (Zoo animals)
    Includes index.
    ISBN 978-0-7614-3144-2
    1. Apes—Juvenile literature. 2. Monkeys—Juvenile literature. I. Pelusey, Jane. II. Title.
    SF408.6.A64P45 2008
    636.98—dc22

                                                                2008001651

Edited by Margaret Maher
Text and cover design by Christine Deering
Page layout by Christine Deering
Illustrations by Gaston Vanzet

Printed in the United States

Acknowledgments
Michael and Jane Pelusey would like to thank Perth Zoo, Melbourne Zoo,
Werribee Wildlife Zoo, and Taronga Zoo for their assistance during this project.

Cover photograph: A mother orangutan shares fruit with her baby, courtesy of Pelusey Photography.

All photographs © Pelusey Photography except for Perth Zoo, **7** (bottom right), **20** (top right); Photodisc/Photolink; **21**; Taronga Zoo, **17**; Derek Smith, **18, 19**.

1 3 5 6 4 2

Contents

Glossary words
When a word is printed in **bold**, you can look up its meaning in the Glossary on page 31.

Zoos

Zoos are places where animals that are usually **wild** are kept in **enclosures**. Some zoos have a lot of space for animals to move about. They are often called wildlife zoos.

A wildlife zoo has a lot of space for large animals to roam.

Zoo Animals

Zoos keep all kinds of animals. People go to zoos to learn about animals. Some animals may become **extinct** if left to live in the wild.

Zookeepers can help people learn about the animals at a zoo.

Apes and Monkeys

Apes and monkeys are **primates**. They are very intelligent. Apes are bigger than monkeys. Monkeys have tails, and apes do not have tails.

A gorilla does not have a tail.

A spider monkey has a thick tail.

There are many kinds of apes and monkeys. They range from the big gorilla to the small pygmy marmoset.

A gorilla is a large ape.

An orangutan is a medium-sized ape.

A baboon is a large monkey.

A chimpanzee is a small ape.

A pygmy marmoset is a small monkey.

In the Wild

In the wild, apes live in Asia and Africa. Apes and monkeys usually live in forests.

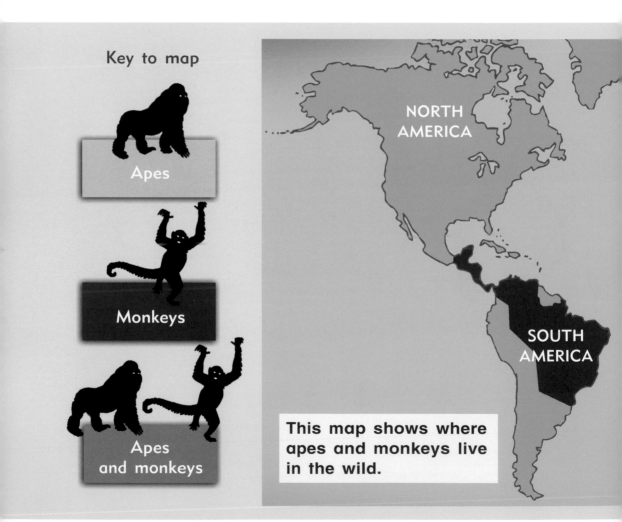

Key to map

Apes

Monkeys

Apes and monkeys

NORTH AMERICA

SOUTH AMERICA

This map shows where apes and monkeys live in the wild.

Wild monkeys live in Asia, Africa, North America, and South America.

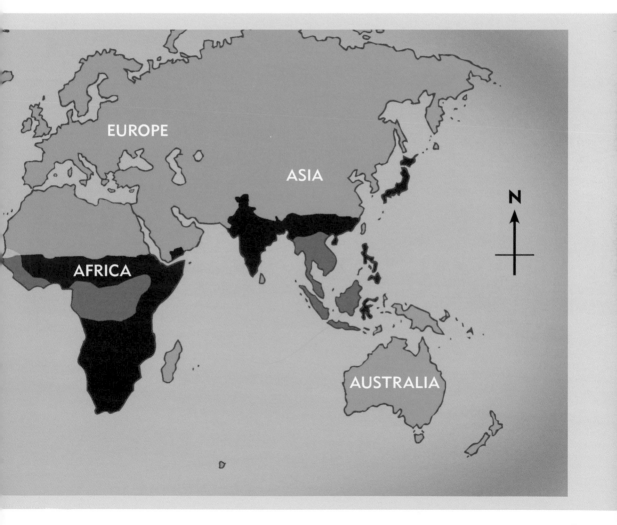

Threats to Survival

The biggest threat to survival for apes and monkeys is forest clearing.

Apes and monkeys cannot survive without forests to live in.

Forests are cleared for timber and farming. This leaves fewer places for apes and monkeys to live.

This forest in Thailand is being cleared for farming.

Zoo Homes

In zoos, apes and monkeys live in enclosures. Enclosures are often like the apes' and monkeys' homes in the wild.

containers for treats

platform to sleep on

ropes to climb

tower to climb

water to drink

The orangutan enclosure has things to climb, like in a forest.

Monkeys, such as baboons, like lots of rocks and tree branches to climb on.

ropes to climb

trees to climb

shade

rocks to climb

This enclosure has lots of things for the baboon to climb.

Zoo Food

Apes and monkeys need to eat different types of food to stay healthy.

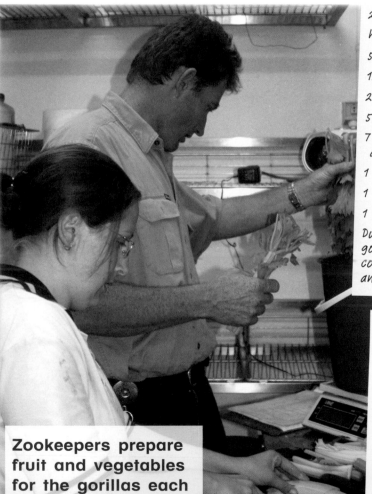

Zookeepers prepare fruit and vegetables for the gorillas each day.

A gorilla's zoo food

2 pounds (1 kg) broccoli

half a cabbage

5 bell peppers

13 pounds (6 kg) celery

2 bunches of **chicory**

5½ lettuces

7 ounces (200 g) peas and beans

1 bunch scallions

1 bunch spinach

1 vitamin C tablet

During the week, give the gorillas extras, such as corn, coconuts, cheese, rhubarb, and fruit.

An orangutan's zoo food

9 pounds (4 kg) vegetables, such as cucumber, corn, sweet potato, zucchini, beetroot, lettuce, and celery

1 pound (500 g) fruit, such as apricots, melon, oranges, and apples

Sometimes, give the orangutans bread, rice, cooked chicken, or popcorn.

Feeding

Apes and monkeys have up to five meals a day. The gorillas' food is often hidden so that they spend time looking for it. This helps entertain the gorillas.

A zookeeper gives an orangutan an extra treat of fruit.

Zoo Health

Zookeepers look after the everyday health of apes and monkeys. They watch carefully to see if the animals are moving well and eating their food.

A zookeeper watches a gorilla to check that it is healthy.

If an ape gets sick, it is visited by the **veterinarian**. Apes are big, strong animals. They need to be **tranquilized** before the veterinarian examines them.

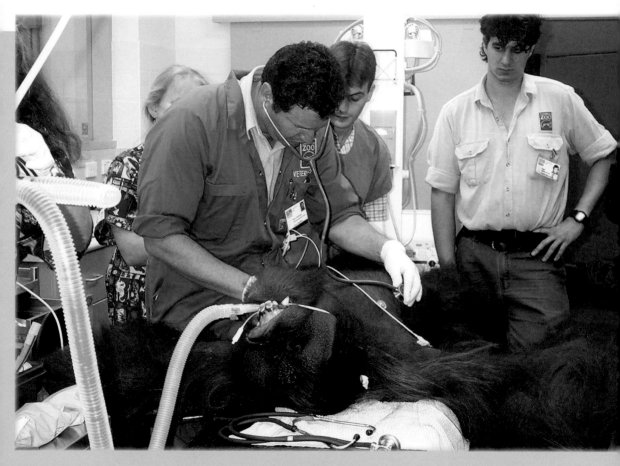

A veterinarian examines a tranquilized orangutan to make sure it is healthy.

Baby Apes and Monkeys

Apes and monkeys have one or two babies at a time. It takes seven to eight months for a baby ape or monkey to grow inside its mother.

This baboon has one baby.

Baby apes and monkeys learn from their mothers. They also learn by copying and playing with other apes and monkeys.

A baby orangutan is taught to climb by its mother.

How Zoos Are Saving Apes and Monkeys

Zoos help save apes and monkeys by **breeding** them. Silvery gibbons, gorillas, and orangutans are **endangered** apes.

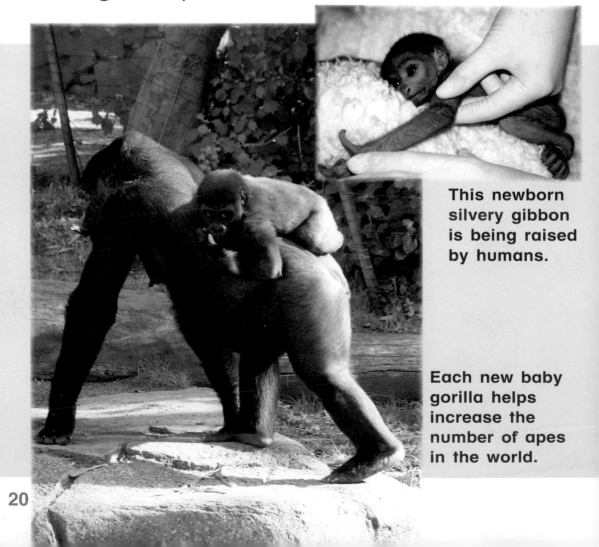

This newborn silvery gibbon is being raised by humans.

Each new baby gorilla helps increase the number of apes in the world.

Many organizations save apes and monkeys in the wild. The Orangutan Foundation International helps to prevent forest clearing where orangutans live. This organization was started by a scientist.

Orangutans can live safely in a protected forest.

Zoos around the world work together. A male gorilla was born in a zoo in England. He was moved to an Australian zoo that needed a male gorilla for breeding.

This male gorilla will now breed in Australia.

The Silvery Gibbon Project helps protect the endangered silvery gibbon. Some zoos teach orangutans to paint pictures. These paintings can be sold to raise money for the Silvery Gibbon Project.

Zoos breed silvery gibbons to increase their numbers in the world.

Meet Andrea, a Gorilla Keeper

Andrea prepares a treat of grapes for the gorillas.

Question How did you become a zookeeper?

Answer I studied science at college and did voluntary work with animals.

Question How long have you been a keeper?

Answer I have been a keeper for four years.

Andrea throws food around the gorilla enclosure.

Question   What other animals have you worked with?

Answer   I have worked with elephants, pygmy hippopotamuses, chimpanzees, and birds.

Question   What do you like about your job?

Answer   I love working with gorillas because they are so intelligent.

A Day in the Life of a Zookeeper

Zookeepers have certain jobs to do each day. Some keepers work with apes and monkeys. The orangutans are looked after by a team of keepers.

8:00 a.m.

Clean the orangutan enclosure while the orangutans are still in their beds.

9:30 a.m.

Release the orangutans into the enclosure.

12:30 p.m.

Prepare food for the orangutans.

3:00 p.m.

Hide jam and other treats around the enclosure to keep the orangutans happy and active.

Zoos Around the World

There are many zoos around the world. The Singapore Zoo has one of the biggest orangutan enclosures. Twenty-four orangutans live in this enclosure. It has tall **rain forest** trees and high platforms.

This orangutan lives with her baby in the Singapore Zoo.

The breeding program at the Singapore Zoo has raised more than thirty-three baby orangutans. When they are old enough, the baby orangutans are sent to zoos in other countries.

One day, this baby orangutan will be sent to live at a different zoo.

The Importance of Zoos

Zoos do very important work. They:

- help people learn about animals
- save endangered animals and animals that are treated badly

With the help of zoos, the orangutan population may increase in the future.

Glossary

breeding   keeping animals so that they can produce babies

chicory   a type of herb

enclosures   the fenced areas where animals are kept in zoos

endangered   at a high risk of becoming extinct

extinct   no longer living on Earth

primates   members of the animal family that includes apes, monkeys, and humans

rain forest   thick forest where the rainfall is high

tranquilized   given a drug that makes the animal unconscious

veterinarian   a doctor who treats animals

wild   living in its natural environment and not taken care of by humans

Index